Hidden *Michigan*

Written by **Anne Margaret Lewis** *and* **Janis Campbell**
Illustrated by **Wendy Popko**

Mackinac Island Press

for the love of reading

Acknowledgements

With special thanks to the many people who shared their knowledge of the great state of Michigan with us. A special thanks to Beth VanHouten for her endless research on this project. As with any writing project, we didn't have room to include so much of what we learned but we enjoyed talking with all of you and thank you for your time and enthusiasm.

Allison Tribul of Kellogg's Cereal City USA, Bill Bonner & Carolyn Curtis of Pointe Aux Barques Lighthouse Society, Bob D'Amelio at Western Michigan University, Cadillac Area Visitors Bureau, Carla Freed of University Relations at Michigan State University, Chelsea Chamber of Commerce, Chris Kull of Monroe County Historical Museum, Courtney Bates, Communications Assistant at Michigan Department of Transportation (MDOT), Debra Polich of Artrain USA, Explore Michigan Traverse City, published by Petoskey Publishing, Isle Royale National Park, Jeanne Lipe of the Michigan Department of Agriculture, Keewenaw Convention and Visitors Bureau, Kellie Mowery of Cabela's, Ken Hayward, Vice President of Sales and Marketing at the Grand Hotel, Kerry Chartkoff, building historian and tour guide director, Capitol Tour Services of the Michigan State Capitol, Lori Schuh, Executive Director of the Clare County Convention & Visitors Bureau, Lynn Yates and Paul Saginaw of Zingerman's, Maria Bronner Sutorik of Bronner's, Mary Carroll, Executive Director of Mount Pleasant Area Convention & Visitors Bureau, Mary Ridderman of the Kalamazoo County Convention & Visitors Bureau, Norman Kent Productions, Northern Michigan Almanac, published by Petoskey Publishing, Pam Smith of the Ann Arbor Hands-On Museum, Patti Cornwell of Cornwell's Turkeyville USA, Porcupine Mountain Wilderness State Park, Robin Kolehmainen of Michigan Technological University, Rogers City Chamber of Commerce, Sandy Schultz of Chelsea Milling Company, Jiffy Mix, Sean Ley of the Great Lakes Shipwreck Museum, Stacy Simmer of Central Michigan University, Tahquamenon Falls State Park, and Tom Sellers of the Clare County Historical Society.

You can learn more great facts about Michigan at the state's official web site, *www.Michigan.gov*

First Edition

Library of Congress Cataloging-in-Publication Data (on file)

Lewis, Anne Margaret, Campbell, Janis, and Popko, Wendy
Hidden Michigan

Summary: Michigan has many different things to do and learn about.

ISBN 1-934133-01-9
ISBN 13   978-1-934133-0-19
Fiction

10 9 8 7 6 5 4 3 2 1

Printed and bound in Canada by Friesens, Altona, Manitoba

A Mackinac Island Press, Inc. publication
Traverse City, Michigan
www.mackinacislandpress.com

To all of the loyal Michiganders,
and a special welcome to visitors and newcomers to
our amazing and breathtaking state

—*Anne Margaret Lewis*

For my travel companions Steve, Andrew, and Colin

—*J.C.*

For my daughter Ashley

—*Wendy Popko*

You have entered the world of
Hidden Michigan!

Explore each region of Michigan in the most creative and entertaining way. Here are some hints for looking for the hidden items on every page, and if you have trouble make sure to look on the Hidden Michigan answer key in the back of the book.

- *Don't be afraid to turn the book every which way. Some things are not right-side-up.*
- *Hold the page up to a mirror to see the image.*
- *If you see something within something else, you have probably found one of the hidden items. Good job!*
- *If it's a 'word' in the hidden items, that's exactly what you are looking for.*

Also hidden on every page:

MICHIGAN *& 2* maps

Make sure to go back and look!

Did you find our hot air balloon on every page?

Before you go, take one minute and find hidden items on the cover of the book: a robin, a lighthouse, a bear, a sailboat, the capitol building, a car, and a turtle.

HAVE FUN!

Detroiters are proud that civil rights activist Rosa Parks came to call Detroit her home. She made history in 1955 when she refused to give up her seat on a bus in Montgomery, Alabama. Mrs. Parks moved to Detroit in 1957. The bus she made famous is now part of an exhibit at The Henry Ford in Dearborn.

Detroit is the largest city in Michigan and used to be our states capital. Can you guess why it's called the Motor City?

The Motor City installed the very first traffic light in the United States in 1915 at the corner of Woodward and Michigan Avenues.

Detroit has a sound all its own! Motown Records was born here but the original Hitsville U.S.A. studio is now the Motown Historical Museum.

The Spirit of Detroit statue has become quite a sports fan. The statue has sported giant jerseys of the city's winning teams, including Red Wings, Pistons, Shock and Tigers jerseys. Talk about hometown spirit!

Hey, there's Clownie! Detroit's Thanksgiving Parade has been a holiday tradition since 1926. The Parade uses 550 cans of adhesive spray or glue on their floats—enough to glue down the artificial turf of a football field. Now that's a lot of glue!

Some MUST SEES!
The Henry Ford Museum and Greenfield Village in Dearborn and The Detroit Science Center in Detroit.

The Cultural Center area near Wayne State University is the place to go if you want to visit some of the best and biggest museums in the United States.

Search for—

Football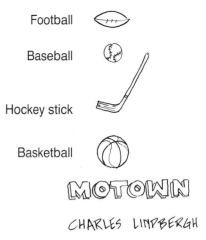

Baseball

Hockey stick

Basketball

MOTOWN

CHARLES LINDBERGH

Motor city magic

The Motor City is full of museums and magic, and home to the famous MOTOWN. There's science and spirit and plenty of sports, come see The Parade's Clownie the Clown!

Search for —

🍪 Cheese

🫧 Ornament

🐟 Fish

🚧 Construction Barrel

🛍 Shopping bag

ZILWAUKEE

A drive up 75

Take a drive up 75,
if vacation is what you seek.
Where you go is up to you;
stay a day or stay a week.

I-75 not only stretches across Michigan from top to bottom, it keeps right on going all the way to Hialeah, Florida, our sunshine state.

If you want to see something special, plant yourself in the beautiful Hartwick Pines State Park in Grayling. The state park, filled with majestic white pines, is one of the largest in the Lower Peninsula covering nearly 10,000 acres.

DOW GARDENS

ZILWAUKEE

Answer riddle to cross the Tridge

The Birch Run outlet malls are the largest in the state. If you love to shop, make time to stop!

Frankenmuth is nicknamed "Michigan's Little Bavaria." Every year three million visitors flock to the town for the charming architecture and famous chicken dinners. Yum!

FRANKENMUTH
Bronner's Birch Run

HOLLY MI
Renaissance Fest

MICHIGAN

PIP-UP TOWN

PINCONNING

FLINT
Robert T. Longway
Planetarium

Why did the chicken cross I-75?

Calling all noble lords and ladies! Step back in time at the annual Michigan Renaissance Festival in Holly.

One of the most famous spots in Midland is "The Tridge," a three-way foot bridge in the downtown area. Local folks like to say friendly trolls live under the bridge, so beware if you visit!

Here's a fact you'll dig: Monroe County is the state leader in registered archaeological sites.

Moo Michigan!
Our state is the 8th largest producer of milk, with two of the top five milk producing counties in the Thumb area.

Reasons to drink milk

Inventor Thomas Alva Edison called Port Huron home when he was a young boy. Edison took a job as a "candy butcher" where he sold candy and newspapers on the Grand Trunk Railroad, servicing Port Huron to Detroit. He then began writing, printing, and selling his own paper, making about $10.00 a day. During the ten hour layover between Detroit and Port Huron he would spend his days at the Detroit Public Library reading any book he could get his hands on!

You could say the state has a green thumb, especially in the Thumb area. The Thumb is the top producer of black beans, navy beans, and kidney beans. We're the fourth leading grower of this crunchy crop—CARROTS!

Jump on the Blue Water Bridge and you can drive from Port Huron to Sarnia, Ontario. Shazaam! You're in Canada!

Search for

Picnic basket

Light bulb

Beach ball

Books

Here's a sweet fact:
Michigan is the 4th largest grower
of sugar beets in the United States.
Can you guess what comes
from sugar beets? Sugar!
About 180,000 acres of sugar beets
are grown here.

Pointe Aux Barques
Festival

BAY PORT
Fish Festival

The Pointe Aux Barques
Lighthouse and Museum in Port Hope
was the home of Michigan's first female
lighthouse keeper, Catherine Shook, who served
from 1849 to 1851. She was only the second female
lighthouse keeper in the United States.

Thumbs up!

More than 120 unique lighthouses
stand guard along the state's
shoreline, more than
any other state.

Get your paper! Read all about it!
The Thumb's the 8th largest producer of milk.
We've got lighthouses and sandy beaches;
and bushels of veggies to be filled.

Search for—

 Wolverine

Dinosaur footprint

Eagle

JIFFY

Go blue!

Boasting of music, spirit, and the great Maize and Blue,
the southeast of Michigan's got oodles to do;
with art fairs, museums and the famed Zingerman's deli,
great history, techno-savvy, and Jiffy muffins for your belly.

Ann Arbor was founded in 1824 by John Allen and Elisha Rumsey and was named in honor of their two wives Ann and Mary Ann.

Founded in 1817 the University of Michigan was one of the first public universities in the nation. In 1837 they moved from Detroit to Ann Arbor, and are one of the the top ten Universities in the country.

MICHIGAN STADIUM
Est. 1817
GO BLUE!

The University of Michigan had its share of astronauts: Jack Lousma, James Irwin, David Scott, and Al Worden.

Did you find the dinosaur footprint? Mastodon bones and dinosaur footprints were found in Saline and can now be seen at the Natural History Museum in Ann Arbor.

Purple Rose Theater

DEXTER CIDER MILL INC.

You can find Michigan's oldest running Cider Mill in Dexter.

Approximately 500,000 people visit the Annual Plymouth International Ice Sculpture Spectacular where carvers from all over the world come to create frozen visions for all to see. COOL!

Did you know that the black and white striped shirt worn by all referees in sports was designed by Lloyd Olds, a graduate of Eastern Michigan University?

Pizza, Pizza!!! In 1960 Tom Monaghan and his brother James borrowed $500.00 to purchase a pizza store in Ypsilanti and this was the start of the now recognized world leader in pizza delivery—Domino's Pizza.

An Average of 105,000 people attend the Michigan football games. Each local football game in Ann Arbor generates $2.2 million for the local economy.

Eastern Michigan University in Ypsilanti was established in 1849.

Our State Capitol building is something for everyone in Michigan to be proud of. It's one of the most beautiful buildings in the state and is modeled after the U.S. Capitol in Washington, D.C.

The oldest and largest Catalpa tree in Michigan lives on the Capitol grounds. The big beauty is at least 130 years old.

90,000 fourth-graders go to the State Capitol each year. Our State Capitol has the very special honor of being a National Historic Landmark.

MSU has one of the coolest mascots in college sports — Sparty, the muscle-bound Spartan.

The Michigan Coat of Arms, which you might recognize from our state flag, features an elk and a moose over the crest. There are probably thousands of elk and moose hidden in the design of the Capitol building.

Michigan State University was founded in 1855. It was the very first college in the U.S. created to teach about the science and technology of raising crops and animals for food.

The half-inch thick glass floor in the central rotunda is made up of 976 pieces of glass. Look up at the inner dome and you'll see eight painted ladies, looking down from the dome and offering gifts to the visitors of this grand building. Can you guess what their gifts to the citizens of Michigan are?

MSU is the biggest university in Michigan — and one of the largest schools in the country. About 45,000 students attend classes, many living on campus.

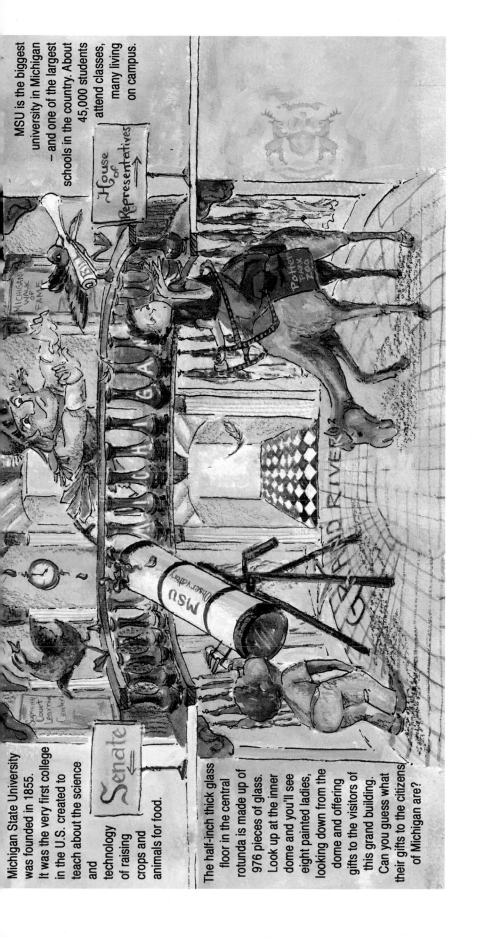

Our cool capital

Lansing is our Capital,
with East Lansing home to MSU.
Come spy some important lawmakers;
and a Sparty, elk or moose.

Search for —

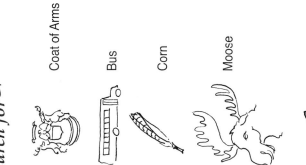

Coat of Arms

Bus

Corn

Moose

GRAND RIVER

Battle Creek is nicknamed the "Cereal City." Why? Because the city is the world leader in producing breakfast cereals.

Battle Creek has been inviting cereal lovers to breakfast each June for five decades. In 1956 the city hosted "The World's Longest Breakfast Table," and serves around 60,000 bowls of free cereal each year.

Here's a tall fact: Battle Creek's Binder Park Zoo has one of the largest giraffe exhibits in the country.

Cornwell's Turkeyville U.S.A. is a famous place in Marshall. The family restaurant began dishing up dinners in 1968. Today, they serve up about 18,000 plates of turkey and stuffing and 30,000 slices of pie each year.

The Air Zoo near Kalamazoo is a colorful place to learn about aviation and space.

The state's very first skateboard park, the K-zoo Skate Zoo doesn't have any wild animals, just wild ramps and runs.

About 80 million pounds of blueberries are grown in Michigan each year, especially in the south-west part of the state. Conditions are perfect for growing strawberries too.

Colon is a magic little place! The tiny town is the largest producer of magic supplies in the world! Don't miss the annual magic festival.

Search for~

Iguana

Flower pot

Peanut

Skateboard

CEREAL CITY

Tastes great!

From Turkeyville to magic land,
Battle Creek to Kalamazoo,
eat blueberries and strawberries, or
spot a giraffe at the Binder Park Zoo.

Search for—

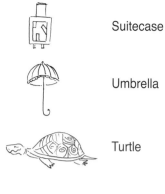

Suitcase

Umbrella

Turtle

Ferry

Back in time

Lilacs, carriage rides, and the miraculous Mighty Mac;
tour the island by bicycle or perhaps on horseback.
Eat some fudge, tour The Grand,
see the historical old Fort.
Come to Mackinaw City, see The Straights,
ride the ferry—All Aboard!

Have you heard of the Straits of Mackinac?
If you look on the map, it's the body of water between
the Lower and Upper Peninsulas, and the place where
Lakes Michigan and Huron come together.
The Mackinac Bridge stretches across the
Straits connecting the two peninsulas.

Mackinac Island is small in size,
but big on history. Visit Fort Mackinac,
built by the British in 1780, and learn
its amazing military past. You might
want to plug your ears for the
cannon-firing demonstrations!

The Mackinac Bridge is nicknamed the "Mighty Mac," and mighty it is. It is five miles long and was the longest suspension bridge in the world when it opened in 1957. In 2007, celebrating its 50th birthday, the bridge is the third longest suspension bridge and will have had more than 100 million cars and trucks make the trip across.

Opening in 1887, the Grand Hotel is a major attraction on Mackinac Island and welcomed its 5 millionth visitor during the summer of 2006. The hotel's 660-foot front porch is the longest in the world. It is decorated with 260 flower boxes and filled with 25,000 Michigan-grown geraniums.

Speaking of Great Lakes, four of the five Great Lakes border our state. Here is a tip to help you remember all five: Think HOMES. That stands for Huron, Ontario, Michigan, Erie and Superior. Only Lake Ontario does not border Michigan.

Are you a Fudgie? Fudge is the favorite souvenir on Mackinac Island. About 15 local fudge makers create thousands of pounds of the sweet stuff every year.

Yummy Fudge

#1 FUDGE

No cars are allowed on Mackinac Island, so you must travel by horse-drawn carriage, bicycle or on foot. There are about 1,800 bicycles on the island and about 500 horses during the summer season.

Kay Ka Kee was originally the name of Clare County but Irish surveyors renamed the area after County Clare in Ireland in 1843. Shamrocks also decorate the street signs and even the local water tower.

The Ziibiwing Center of Anishinabe Culture & Lifeways from the Saginaw Chippewa Indian tribe in Mount Pleasant is a great place to learn about Central Michigan's largest Tribal Nation. The center is one of the largest of its kind in the United States.

Michigan is one of many states that got its name from Native American words. Michigan comes from the word 'Michigama' which means great or large lake.

Clare County is Amish country. If you visit, you might notice horse-drawn buggies traveling down the streets. Many Amish families began setting in Clare from Ohio in the early 1980's.

Can you imagine a million dollar painting hanging on the walls in your school? Clare Middle School has a very special and valuable mural by Grand Rapids artist Gerald Mast on the wall of the school's auditorium. It was painted as part of President Franklin D. Roosevelt's Federal Art Project of the Works Progress Administration in the 1930's.

Can you point out the different Native American dancers? A traditional male dancer, a jingle female dancer, a grass male dancer, fancy male dancer, and a fancy shawl female dancer.

Search for—

Leaf

Quilt

Robin

Kay-Ka-Kee

The enchanted middle

Ah! The luck of the Irish.
Shamrocks splatter an Irish Vibe.
Meet the great Chief Pigeon Hawk,
Chief of the Chippewa Tribe.

Tourism is a big part of central Michigan's economy. Visitors come to Osceola, Clare, Mecosta and Isabella counties to enjoy the many parks, lakes, fishing, golfing and outdoor fun.

Making it on Ripley's Believe It or Not is the canal between Lakes Mitchell and Cadillac. The canal freezes before the lakes, thaws once the lakes are frozen, and stays thawed for the rest of the season.

In 1988 the U.S. Capitol Building Christmas tree was from Cadillac.

Ludington used to be known for its sawmills where in 1892 162 million board feet of lumber and 52 million wood shingles had been produced. Now that's a lot of wood!

Visit the llama farm in Ludington.

If you found the hidden Humpty Dumpty, he represents the famous Humpty-Dumpty folding egg crates that were first designed in Cadillac.

Harriet Quimby, born and schooled in Arcadia, was the first American women to receive an aviation license and the first woman to fly solo over the English Channel.

MANISTEE NATIONAL FOREST →

← LAKE MITCHELL

I RODE THE WATER BUG

Since 1984 Cadillac has hosted the North American Snowmobile Festival with over 137 miles of snowmobile trails.

Hitch a ride on the S.S. Badger from Ludington to Manitowoc, Wisconsin. This is the largest car ferry to ever cruise on Lake Michigan. It carries 620 passengers and 180 automobiles, buses, RV's, and trucks.

The Wreck of the Minnehaha, one of the largest sailing ships on the Great Lakes, sits on the shore of Lake Michigan near Arcadia, Michigan.

Search for —

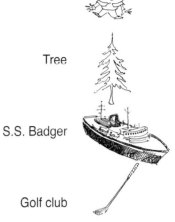

Humpty Dumpty

Tree

S.S. Badger

Golf club

Vacation destination

*Ride the snow or ride the wind,
or catch some fish through a hole in the ice.
Sing songs by the campfire, cook a s'more,
have some fun and don't think twice.*

Into the blue

Welcome to the thrilling
northeast of Michigan;
you'll see sturgeons, lighthouses,
and the Polar Bear Swim.

There are canoe races, sink holes,
and the famous Thunder Bay,
with plenty of shipwrecks to see,
come along, right this way!

Eagles Nest Overlook is one of the most famous overlooks in the Huron National Forest.

Do you think you could make the 120 mile, 14 non-stop hours Weyerhaeuser canoe race? This is the longest non-stop canoe race in North America.

Onaway is the sturgeon capital of Michigan. The sturgeon is one of the oldest species of fish in existence today.

Established in 1908 near Rogers City is the Calcite Plant—the largest limestone quarry in the world. Limestone is a raw mineral essential in making steel, chemicals, and cement.

awas hosts the Annual Winter Festival where more han 200 people attempt the Polar Bear Swim through Tawas Bay, BRRRR!

Oscoda hosts the annual Paul Bunyan Festival.

The Brown Trout Festival In Alpena Is the longest fishing tournament on the Great Lakes.

The Steven's Twin Sinks Preserve in Alpena is where you can see a sink hole 200 feet in diameter and 85 feet deep.

Visit the Thunder Bay National Marine Sanctuary and Underwater Preserve where you can see one of the nation's largest collections of shipwrecks.

YANKEE AIR MUSEUM SHOW!

WORM

Watch you ste Sink Hole

Traverse City was named after Grand Traverse Bay, which was named by French explorers in the 18th century. Traverse City calls itself the Cherry Capital of the World, with the first production of cherries dating back to 1852. Today, Michigan grows about 250 million pounds of tart cherries.

Did you know that Ernest Hemmingway spent the first 18 summers of his life in Petoskey?

The Maritime Academy in Traverse City is the only freshwater maritime academy in the U.S.

Don't miss the Charlevoix Venetian Festival held each year since 1931.

Northern Michigan boasts history, lakes, lighthouses, snow and water skiing, windsurfing, golf, hiking, biking, ice fishing, fishing, great food, and so many great little towns that you'll need several weeks to visit them all.

MICHIGAN

CASTLE FARMS

SUTTON'S BAY

Have you ever climbed the Sleeping Bear Dunes?
Make sure you bring your climbing legs.
The Sleeping Bear Dunes is over 500 feet high
and spans 35 miles of the Lake Michigan coastline.

Founded in 1928, Interlochen Center for the Arts is a community of
students, teachers, alumni, performers, arts patrons, volunteers
and audience drawn from all over the world.

East Jordan Iron Works established in 1883
makes many of the fire hydrants
and manhole covers all over our country.

Raven Hill Discovery Center

Up north

Cherries, sand, and so much snow,
come to the north and see the wind blow!
Skiing, sand castles...hear Mother Bear snore?
What else can you discover in our great outdoors?

Search for~

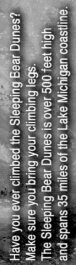

Native American

Fish

Torch

SUTTON'S BAY

Search for —

Kite

Pickle

Luge rider

Windmill

OZ

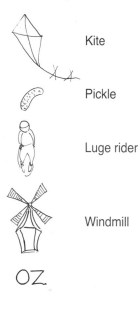

A western voyage

Ride a frog in Meijer Gardens,
eat some pickles, see the zoo,
touch a sting ray, fly a kite,
or wear a pair of dutch shoes!

Watch the windmill,
see the musical fountain, take the Lake Express,
sweep some tulips, spot the Silversides,
join the grand Coast Guard Fest.

Did you find the luge rider? The luge run here at the Muskegon Winter Sports Complex has one of the United States 5 luge runs and serves as an Olympic training site.

Feeling artsy? Visit Blue Lake Fine Arts camp near Muskegon.

Grand Haven, known as Coast Guard City, has the world's largest musical fountain.

How about a sleepover at the Great Lakes Naval Memorial and Museum where the USS Silversides sits? OR, stay overnight on a WWII submarine, or on the 1927 Coast Guard cutter, the USCGC McLane.

Do you want to touch a Sting Ray? Stop off at the Sting Ray Lagoon touch pool at the John Ball Zoo.

You won't want to miss Holland, where you can tiptoe through the five million tulips that bloom each spring. Take a step back in time and visit the DeZwaan Windmill Island where you can see a 240 year old authentic Dutch windmill.

If it's history you seek, then by all means go to the Gerald R. Ford Presidential Museum. Did you know former President Gerald R. Ford wasn't always Gerald R. Ford? He was Leslie Lynch King, Jr. until 1935 when he changed his name.

Don't forget to stop off at the Frederick Meijer Gardens and Sculpture Park in Grand Rapids. Maybe a giant frog sculpture will take you for a ride too!

Heinz USA in Holland has the world's largest pickle factory where over one million pounds of pickles are processed per day.

Mount Baldhead Sand Dune →

Search for—

 Bike

 Moccasin

Wigwam

 Boxing glove

CARPENTER'S DAIRY

On the edge

Come to the edge of Michigan.
Catch a big ship or wave!
See the Maids of the Mist,
some art and even a cave.

Did you know that Muhammed Ali, a three-time World Heavyweight Boxing Champion retired to Berrien Springs? Did you find his boxing glove?

Warren Dunes State Park has dunes up to 260 feet above the lake, an awesome spot for hang gliding!

Pick a fruit, any fruit! The Southwest of Michigan is known for their fruit and veggie crops from apples to blueberries, and tomatoes to zucchini. You pick it! You eat it!

For all of you tractor lovers, a trip to the Michigan Flywheelers Museum is a must!

Beware of BEAR CAVE! At this unique and natural cave you will find stalactites, flowstone, and even petrified leaves. Not too scary, just FUN!

You can spot some 300 cows at The Carpenter's Dairy Farm where nearly 2 million pounds of milk are produced.

The Blossomtime Festival was established in 1906 in Benton Harbor.

Did you find the moccasin? Did you know that as early as 6300 B.C. first inhabitants lived at Moccasin Bluff?

Peninsula Point Lighthouse is the migration point for Monarch butterflies before they go to the Door Peninsula.

Whitefish Point is also known as a migration corridor for more than 300 species of birds.

Pictured Rocks was designated as America's 1st National Lakeshore in 1966 with its shallow caves, arches, and castle turrets and spans 12 miles.

MICHIGAN

Look for the International Bridge, a steel truss arch bridge, built in 1962 to connect Sault St. Marie, Michigan to Sault St. Marie, Ontario spanning 2.8 miles long. How many rulers do you think that equals?

GIPPER LOGGING

CONTEST

Life in the 19th Century in the U.P. revolved around mining and logging. Visit the authentic Delaware Copper Mine for a tour. Started in 1847, it was 1400 feet below ground where over eight million pounds of Copper was mined.

In 1855 the Soo Locks opened its waterways to vessels carrying iron ore, limestone, coal, grain, cement, salt, and sand. The U.P. produced more mineral wealth than the California Gold Rush because it simplified shipping.

Whitefish Point is the oldest active lighthouse on Lake Superior and marks the 80 mile stretch of coast known as Lake Superior's Shipwreck Coast.

The Soo Locks raise and lower the ships 21 feet from the St. Mary's rapids to Lake Superior. More than 11,000 vessels carrying more than 90 million tons of cargo pass through these locks each year, the busiest in the world.

Search for —

Pick ax

Campfire

Freighter

U.P

Hiker

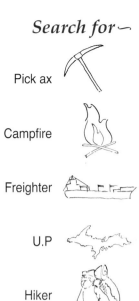

The U.P. – a gold mine

Copper mining and logging and shipwrecks, OH MY!
Bears eating maple syrup and thimbleberry pie.
Lighthouses, the Soo and castles at Pictured Rocks,
discover Monarch butterflies migrating by the flocks.

There are over 150 waterfalls in Michigan including the Tahquamenon Falls. The Upper Falls are more than 200 feet across and drain as much as 50,000 gallons of water per second. The amber colors you see running down the falls comes from the tannin produced from the Spruce, Cedar, and Hemlock trees.

The Upper Peninsula (U.P.) boasts of hunting, fishing, hiking, kayaking, camping, and many more fun things to do. Nature is the U.P.'s playground.

Talk about old—the Porcupine Mountains are one of the oldest mountain chains in the world with Summit Point its highest peak at 1958 feet. It has trees over 200 years old. The Wilderness State Park was established in 1945 to oversee their protection. At that age they deserve to be protected!

Newberry is the moose capital of Michigan.

ISLE ROYALE

BROCKWAY MOUNTAIN DRIVE CAFE

NEW! SENIOR TREE 99¢ a lb.

Pasties

Search for —

Fish

Porcupine

Snowshoe

Buck

Wolf

The National Ski Hall of Fame and Copper Peak Ski Jump are located in the U.P. This is the largest ski jump in the world – 176 feet above the top of the hill.

The largest island in Lake Superior is Isle Royale. It has many wolves and moose and was formed from ancient lava flows and glaciers. Greenstone Ridge is the mainstay of Isle Royale and is thought to be part of one of the largest lava flows on earth!

The Keweenaw Peninsula is not only known as the snow capital of the Midwest with almost 400 inches per year, but is also home to the Estivant Pines Sanctuary – home to the oldest living trees in Michigan.

What's U.P. beautiful?

Fishing and waterfalls and so much snow,
moose and deer and porcupine mountains, OH NO!
Wolves and ski jumps and so much to see—
explore the old forests to meet grandfather tree.
Welcome, welcome to the GREAT, GREAT U.P.!

My Michigan symbols

State Gem – *Chlorastrolite*
State Nickname – *Wolverine State*
State Mammal – *White-tailed deer*
State Wildflower – *Dwarf Lake Iris*
State Song – *Michigan, My Michigan*
State Motto – *If you seek a pleasant peninsula, look about you*

If you seek a pleasant peninsula,

Wolverine State

Michigan, My Michigan

look about you.

State Bird – Robin
State Reptile – Painted turtle
State Fish – Brook trout
State Flower – Apple blossom
State Tree – White pine
State Soil – Kalkaska sand
State Stone – Petoskey Stone

Hidden Michigan answer key

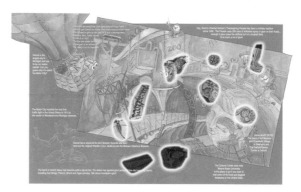

Motor City Magic

A Drive Up 75

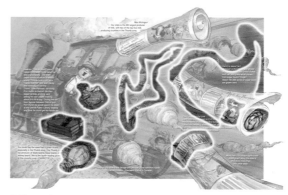

Thumbs Up!

Go Blue!

Our Cool Capital

Tastes Great!

Back In Time

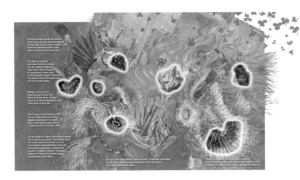

The Enchanted Middle

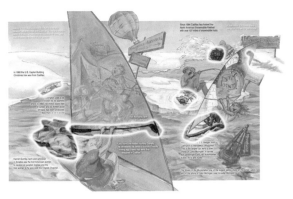

Vacation Destination

Into The Blue

Up North

A Western Voyage

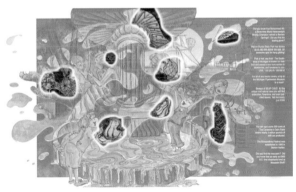

On The Edge

The U.P. – A Gold Mine

What's U.P. Beautiful?

Congratulations! You made it,
from Detroit to the great U.P.
We hope you enjoyed *Hidden Michigan,*
and saw everything in between.